Unlocking Entrepreneurial Success:

Mastering the Art of Building Profitable Ventures"

Victor M. Berta

copyright massage

Appendix

Additional resources and tools

Worksheets and templates for real application

Introduction:

In the vast landscape of business, where dreams of success clash with the realities of challenges, lies the realm of entrepreneurship - a thrilling journey of creativity, determination, and tenacity. It is a road trodden by visionaries, risk-takers, and dream-chasers, each looking to carve their mark in the world through their ingenuity and enterprise. Welcome to "Unlocking Entrepreneurial Success," a transformative exploration of what it truly means to start on the entrepreneurial journey.

As we step into the pages of this book, we start on a journey that is both inspirational and practical, meant to empower aspiring and seasoned entrepreneurs alike. Here, we delve deep into the heart of entrepreneurship, showing the secrets that unlock the doors to lasting success. We aim to nurture the entrepreneurial spirit, ignite a passion for innovation, and provide the tools needed to beat the hurdles that inevitably lie ahead.

Chapter by chapter, we will unlock the keys to entrepreneurial success - from developing a resilient mindset to mastering the art of adaptation and embracing the power of failure. Through the stories of accomplished entrepreneurs who have weathered the storms of uncertainty, we gain invaluable insights and learn from their successes and tribulations.

Part I: The Heart of Entrepreneurship

In Part I, we lay the foundation for our journey by learning the heart and essence of entrepreneurship. We study the power of passion and purpose, delving into the driving forces that ignite the spark of innovation. Unearthing one's real calling and aligning it with business aspirations sets the stage for a transformative entrepreneurial endeavour.

Part II: Embracing the Risks and Challenges

Entrepreneurship is not without its risks and challenges, and in Part II, we face these head-on. We explore the art of calculated risk-taking, understanding that uncertainty can be both a powerful foe and a wellspring of opportunity. In this part, we unveil strategies to handle adversity, tackle setbacks, and forge ahead with unwavering determination.

Part III: The Innovation Imperative

At the core of business success lies the spirit of innovation, and in Part III, we explore the fertile grounds of creativity and ideation. We learn to identify gaps in the market, build value-driven solutions, and navigate the ever-evolving landscape of innovation. We hear from trailblazing entrepreneurs who changed industries, challenging the status quo with audacious ideas.

Part IV: Nurturing Growth and Resilience

As the business journey unfolds, so do the lessons in growth and resilience. In Part IV, we discover the art of scaling projects, expanding reach, and embracing growth without losing sight of the core values that define success. We also discover the strength that lies in resilience, the ability to bounce back from setbacks and emerge stronger and more determined.

Part V: Sustaining Success and Leaving a Legacy

Our trip reaches its zenith in Part V, where we dig into the significance of sustaining success and leaving a lasting legacy. We explore the transformative power of purpose-driven entrepreneurship, making a meaningful effect on society and leaving the world a better place.

Unlocking Entrepreneurial Success is not just a roadmap to financial success; it is a transformative guide that nurtures the spirit of entrepreneurship from within. It is a tribute to the brave hearts who dare to dream, those who believe in their potential to create something special. Within these pages, we embrace the challenges, savour the triumphs, and reveal the secrets to unlocking the full potential of entrepreneurial success.

Join us as we start on this transformative journey, where the spirit of innovation meets the power of resilience, and entrepreneurial dreams are turned into reality. Whether you are a budding entrepreneur eager to take your first steps or a seasoned business leader wanting renewed motivation, Unlocking Entrepreneurial Success is your compass, guiding you through the turbulent yet rewarding waters of entrepreneurship.

PART ONE

Identifying a Profitable Market Gap

In the ever- evolving geography of business and entrepreneurship, the key to success frequently lies in relating and staking on untapped openings within the request. This process is generally known as relating to a profitable request gap. It involves feting unmet requirements, underserved client parts, or areas with limited competition, and strategically situating a product or service to feed to these voids. By uncovering these gaps, entrepreneurs can place themselves for sustainable growth, isolation, and success in a competitive business.

The first step in relating to a profitable request gap is conducting comprehensive request exploration. This involves gathering and assaying data to gain perceptivity into consumer geste

, preferences, and pain points. Entrepreneurs must immerse themselves in their target request, understanding the challenges faced by guests and the failings of being products or services. Through checks, focus groups, interviews, and observation, they can discern trends and unfulfilled demands that may hold the key to an economic request occasion.

The coming stage involves critically assaying the data collected during the exploration phase. Entrepreneurs must objectively assess the eventuality of each gap they discover. Some gaps may be too niche or short- lived to support a sustainable business, while others may offer significant long- term eventuality. This logical process requires an open mind and an amenability to acclimatise one's original ideas to the realities of the request.

Once a promising request gap is linked, the entrepreneur must define their target followership easily. Understanding the characteristics, requirements, and preferences of the ideal client is pivotal for casting a product or service that precisely addresses their pain points. Effective request segmentation allows for acclimatised marketing strategies and better communication with implicit guests, adding the chances of success.

Creating a value proposition that resonates with the target followership is the coming pivotal step in filling a request gap profitably. The value proposition should easily articulate the unique benefits that the product or service offers to guests and how it stands out from challengers. A compelling value proposition instills confidence in implicit guests and motivates them to choose the new immolation over being druthers

.

One way to validate the viability of the linked request gap is through a minimal feasible product(MVP) approach. By developing a simplified interpretation of the product or service, entrepreneurs can test its appeal and functionality in the real request. Feedback from early adopters will give precious perceptivity into product- request fit and help upgrade the immolation before full- scale perpetration.

Also, continuously covering request trends and client feedback is essential to stay ahead in an ever- changing request terrain. requests are dynamic, and consumer preferences can shift fleetly. Entrepreneurs must remain nimble and adaptable to seize new openings or pivot their business model when necessary.

Eventually, it's essential to fete that relating a profitable request gap isn't a one- time event. Successful entrepreneurs understand that request dynamics are constantly evolving, and the process of relating new gaps and innovative results is ongoing. Embracing a culture of invention and fostering a creative mindset will insure the sustainability and long- term growth of the adventure.

In conclusion, relating a profitable request gap is a foundational element of entrepreneurial success. Through rigorous request exploration, objective analysis, and client- centric approaches, entrepreneurs can uncover openings that align with their heartstrings and strengths while meeting the unmet requirements of consumers. By continuously repeating, conforming, and evolving, they can make gambles that not only thrive in the present but also shape the future of diligence and requests.

1.Market Research and Analysis:

Unveiling the Secrets to Informed Decision-Making

Request exploration and analysis serve as the bedrock of successful business gambles. It's a comprehensive process that involves gathering, interpreting, and assessing data to gain perceptivity into request dynamics, client geste , and assiduity trends. By employing these logical tools, businesses can make informed opinions, identify openings, alleviate pitfalls, and knitter their strategies to meet the requirements of their target followership effectively.

The first step in request exploration is defining the compass and objects of the study. Whether an incipiency exploring new requests or an established company launching a new product, clarity in pretensions is consummate. This sets the direction for the exploration and ensures that sweats are concentrated on applicable areas, precluding resource destruction.

Primary and secondary exploration are two abecedarian approaches used in request exploration. Primary exploration involves collecting firsthand data directly from the target followership. This can be achieved through checks, focus groups, interviews, or observation. On the other hand, secondary exploration involves exercising data from colourful sources, similar as government publications, assiduity reports, and academic studies. A combination of both approaches provides a comprehensive and well- rounded view of the request.

Quantitative and qualitative styles are generally used in primary exploration. Quantitative data, expressed in numerical terms, allows for statistical analysis and objective conclusions. checks and questionnaires are exemplifications of quantitative styles. Qualitative data, on the other hand, provides a deeper understanding of consumer geste

and preferences. It involves gathering private information through open- concluded questions, interviews, or concentrate groups.

To ensure the delicacy and trustability of the data collected, experimenters must pay attention to the sample size and slice system. A representative sample that directly reflects the characteristics of the target population is pivotal for drawing meaningful perceptivity. Random slice, stratified slice, and convenience slice are some of the common ways used to elect samples.

Once data is collected, it undergoes analysis to prize meaningful patterns and perceptivity. Data analysis ways can vary depending on the type of data and exploration objects. Quantitative data is frequently anatomized using statistical software to identify trends, correlations, and patterns. Qualitative data requires a more interpretive approach to uncover themes and sentiments.

One of the essential aspects of request exploration and analysis is contender analysis. Understanding the competitive geography is pivotal for businesses to identify their strengths, sins, and unique selling points. By assessing challengers' products, pricing, marketing strategies, and request share, businesses can identify gaps in the request or areas for enhancement.

Request exploration not only helps identify openings but also assists in mollifying pitfalls. By understanding request trends and implicit challenges, businesses can proactively acclimate their strategies to navigate misgivings effectively. It allows them to be more nimble and responsive to changes in the business terrain.

Also, request exploration plays a vital part in product development and invention. By collecting client feedback and preferences, businesses can upgrade their products or services to meet client requirements. This client- centric approach increases the chances of success in the request.

In conclusion, request exploration and analysis are necessary tools for businesses seeking success in a competitive world. The data- driven perceptivity gained from this process empower decision- makers to make informed choices, seize openings, and knitter their strategies to the ever- changing request geography. By understanding their guests, challengers, and assiduity trends, businesses can place themselves for growth, profitability, and long- term success.

2. Recognizing Unmet Needs and Opportunities:

The Pathway to Innovation and Success.

In the realm of entrepreneurship and business, identifying unmet needs and opportunities is the driving force behind groundbreaking innovations and remarkable success stories. This process involves keen observation, empathy, and a deep understanding of customer pain points and desires. By recognizing these unaddressed gaps in the market, entrepreneurs can unlock the potential for creating products or services that meet genuine customer needs, paving the way for differentiation, growth, and lasting impact.

The first step in recognizing unmet needs and opportunities is to closely observe and listen to customers. Understanding their experiences, frustrations, and aspirations allows entrepreneurs to identify pain points and areas where current solutions fall short. This empathetic approach enables them to develop a deeper connection with their target audience, fostering trust and loyalty.

Customer feedback is a valuable source of information in this process. Surveys, focus groups, and direct interactions provide valuable insights into what customers want and what they wish existed. Paying attention to customer reviews, comments on social media, and suggestions helps uncover hidden opportunities and areas for improvement.

Another avenue for identifying unmet needs is to analyze trends and developments in the industry. Keeping a close eye on technological advancements, societal shifts, and changes in consumer behavior can lead to the discovery of emerging needs and opportunities. Being at the forefront of such trends allows entrepreneurs to be proactive in meeting future demands.

To fully understand unmet needs and opportunities, entrepreneurs must step outside their comfort zones and explore different perspectives. This involves looking beyond their immediate industry or sector to gain inspiration from unrelated fields. Cross-industry learning often sparks innovative ideas and novel solutions that can be adapted to solve problems in new and creative ways.

Market research plays a pivotal role in recognizing unmet needs and opportunities. Conducting thorough market analysis helps entrepreneurs identify gaps in the market, assess the demand for potential solutions, and evaluate the feasibility of entering a specific market segment. Market research enables entrepreneurs to make data-driven decisions and minimizes the risk of investing in ventures with limited potential.

Furthermore, networking and engaging with like-minded individuals and professionals can also provide fresh insights and ideas. Collaborating with diverse groups, attending conferences, and participating in industry events create opportunities for brainstorming and sharing knowledge, fostering an environment of innovation and learning.

Innovation is often fueled by the drive to solve real-world problems. Entrepreneurs who focus on recognizing unmet needs and opportunities are not solely driven by profit but by a genuine desire to make a positive impact. This purpose-driven approach resonates with customers, employees, and investors, leading to a stronger brand reputation and a loyal customer base.

In conclusion, recognizing unmet needs and opportunities is the catalyst for entrepreneurial success and innovation. By closely listening to customers, analyzing market trends, and embracing diverse perspectives, entrepreneurs can uncover hidden potential and create solutions that address genuine needs. This customer-centric and purpose-driven approach fosters growth, sets businesses apart from competitors, and ultimately leads to a lasting positive impact on society. Embracing the journey of discovery and constant learning, entrepreneurs can transform challenges into opportunities and shape a future filled with innovation and growth.

PART TWO.

Crafting a Compelling Vision:

The Art of Inspiring and Guiding Success

In the world of business and leadership, crafting a compelling vision serves as a strong beacon, guiding organisations towards their goals and inspiring teams to achieve greatness. A compelling vision goes beyond a simple statement; it requires a deep knowledge of the company's purpose, a clear depiction of the desired future, and the ability to communicate it in a way that resonates with stakeholders. Such a vision not only defines the direction but also ignites passion and commitment among workers, customers, and partners, propelling the company towards success.

At the heart of a compelling vision lies a strong foundation of purpose and ideals. Entrepreneurs and leaders must reflect on why their business exists beyond financial gain. Understanding and articulating the higher purpose that drives the company's mission is important for building a vision that transcends day-to-day operations and aligns with the ambitions of employees and customers alike. A well-defined purpose acts as a guiding compass for decision-making and culture-building, instilling a feeling of meaning and direction into the organisation.

A well-crafted vision paints a clear picture of the ideal future. It is aspirational, inspiring, and ambitious yet doable. Leaders should envision the organisation's effect on the world and communicate it in a way that creates excitement and enthusiasm. The vision should answer the question of "what could be" and motivate workers to aim for excellence, encouraging them to go above and beyond to bring the vision to life.

To make the idea compelling, it must be communicated effectively. Leaders should explain the goal in a clear, concise, and memorable way. Using storytelling techniques can make the goal relatable and emotionally resonant, appealing to the hearts and minds of the audience. Repetition of the vision through various channels and regular support ensures that it becomes ingrained in the organisation's culture and becomes a driving force in decision-making and actions.

Furthermore, a compelling vision supports a feeling of shared ownership and inclusivity. Leaders should involve workers and stakeholders in the vision-building process, encouraging their input and comments. When people feel valuable and part of the vision's creation, they become more committed to its realisation. A vision that promotes collaboration and unity is more likely to be embraced and passionately followed by the entire company.

A visionary leader serves as the champion of the appealing goal. By embodying the vision's beliefs and actions, leaders set an example for others to follow. They must align their actions and choices with the goal and show unwavering dedication to its achievement. Authenticity and trustworthiness are vital in garnering trust and support from workers and stakeholders.

A compelling vision goes beyond a mere marketing method; it becomes the driving force behind strategic planning and resource allocation. It guides the organisation's direction, shapes its culture, and helps prioritise projects that add to the vision's realisation. With a clear vision, employees are empowered to make choices that fit with the organisation's long-term goals, encouraging agility and adaptability in the face of challenges.

As the world changes, so too may the organisation's goal. Leaders must be open to reviewing and refining the vision periodically to ensure its relevance and connection with changing circumstances. A dynamic vision that evolves with the times shows a willingness to accept change and innovation.

In conclusion, creating a compelling vision is an art that requires purpose, foresight, and effective communication. A well-crafted vision energises and mobilises the entire company, aligning efforts towards a shared cause and inspiring everyone to contribute their best. It becomes the driving force that pushes the company towards success, guiding decision-making, fostering teamwork, and instilling a sense of purpose among all stakeholders. With a compelling vision as their north star, organisations can handle the challenges of today and build a better future.

1.Defining Your Startup's Purpose and Mission:

Charting the Course for Success

At the heart of every successful incipiency lies a clear and compelling purpose, backed by a well-defined charge. Defining your incipiency's purpose and charge is further than a superficial exercise; it's the foundational step that shapes the entire line of the adventure. A purpose-driven incipiency not only attracts guests and investors but also motivates workers and fosters a strong company culture. In this vital process, entrepreneurs must introspect, identify their heartstrings, and align their business pretensions with an advanced calling that resonates with stakeholders.

To start, entrepreneurs must look inward and explore their provocations for starting the adventure. They need to ask themselves why they're embarking on this entrepreneurial trip. What problem do they want to break, and what impact do they aspire to make in the world? Understanding their particular values and heartstrings is essential for shaping the purpose of the incipiency. A purpose that's genuine and authentic creates a sense of conviction that shines through in every aspect of the business.

Beyond particular provocations, the purpose of the incipiency should address a real need in the request. It should concentrate on creating value for guests, society, or the terrain. By addressing a genuine problem or occasion, the incipiency's purpose becomes meaningful and applicable to the target followership. This resonance with guests fosters brand fidelity and trust, which are vital for sustainable success.

A well- defined charge complements the purpose, furnishing the roadmap for achieving the incipiency's pretensions. The charge statement should articulate the concrete conduct and strategies the incipiency will take over to fulfil its purpose. It should be specific, measurable, attainable, applicable, and time- bound(SMART). A clear charge statement helps align all sweats towards a common thing and serves as a guiding force for decision- making at every position of the association.

As the incipiency's purpose and charge are developed, it's pivotal to involve crucial stakeholders in the process. This includes co-founders, workers, investors, and indeed implicit guests. cooperative conversations and feedback sessions insure that the purpose and charge reverberate with the entire platoon and are inclusive of different perspectives. When everyone feels a sense of power and connection to the incipiency's purpose, they come more married to its success.

The purpose and charge should be communicated effectively both internally and externally. Internally, regular conversations, shops, and training sessions should support the incipiency's purpose and charge among workers. This creates a sense of purpose- driven culture, motivating workers to go the redundant afar and embody the incipiency's values in their diurnal work.

Externally, the purpose and charge should be communicated through marketing sweats, the company's website, and other public- facing accoutrements . By participating the incipiency's advanced calling with the world, entrepreneurs can attract guests who partake the same values and beliefs. This authentic liar enhances brand fidelity and creates a deeper emotional connection with guests.

A purpose- driven incipiency is more likely to attract investors who align with its values and long- term pretensions. Investors seek startups that not only offer fiscal returns but also contribute appreciatively to society. A clear purpose and charge demonstrate that the incipiency is committed to creating a sustainable impact, making it an seductive investment occasion.

In conclusion, defining your incipiency's purpose and charge is a transformative process that shapes the entire line of the adventure. It's a reflection of the entrepreneur's passion and values, while also addressing a genuine need in the request. A well- defined purpose and charge align the entire association, creating a sense of purpose- driven culture and motivating workers to exceed. By communicating the purpose and charge effectively, startups can attract pious guests and investors who partake in the same values. A purpose- driven incipiency stands piecemeal from the competition, instils trust among stakeholders, and maps the course for long- term success and positive impact.

2. Inspiring a Shared Vision Among Team Members:

Fostering Collaboration and Collective Success

In the realm of effective leadership, inspiring a shared vision among team members is a vital aspect that propels organizations towards greatness. A shared vision unites individuals around a common goal, fostering collaboration, commitment, and a sense of purpose. It empowers team members to work cohesively towards a collective vision, achieving results that go beyond individual efforts. To inspire a shared vision, leaders must communicate their vision authentically, involve team members in the process, and cultivate an environment of trust and empowerment.

The first step in inspiring a shared vision is for the leader to articulate their vision with clarity and passion. The vision should be aspirational and future-oriented, painting a compelling picture of the desired future. Leaders must communicate this vision consistently and authentically, using storytelling techniques that resonate with team members emotionally. By sharing their passion for the vision, leaders ignite enthusiasm and motivate team members to contribute their best efforts towards its realization.

Involving team members in the vision-building process is crucial for creating a shared sense of ownership and commitment. Leaders should actively seek input and feedback from team members, making them feel valued and part of the decision-making process. Collaborative discussions, brainstorming sessions, and open forums allow diverse perspectives to be considered, leading to a more comprehensive and inclusive vision.

Effective leaders create opportunities for team members to connect with the vision on a personal level. They demonstrate how each individual's contribution aligns with the overall vision and how their work makes a meaningful impact. By connecting team members' day-to-day tasks to the broader purpose, leaders instill a sense of purpose-driven motivation, fostering a greater sense of meaning and fulfillment in their roles.

To inspire a shared vision, leaders must lead by example and demonstrate their unwavering commitment to the vision. Consistency between words and actions builds trust and credibility. When team members see their leader actively working towards the vision, they are more likely to follow suit, embodying the values and principles that underpin the shared vision.

Moreover, creating a collaborative and supportive team culture is essential for nurturing a shared vision. Leaders should encourage open communication, where team members feel comfortable sharing ideas, asking questions, and providing constructive feedback. Trust and psychological safety within the team foster an environment where everyone feels empowered to contribute and take ownership of the shared vision.

Celebrating small wins and milestones along the way is essential for sustaining motivation and momentum. Recognizing team members' efforts and accomplishments reinforces the connection between individual contributions and the shared vision. This positive reinforcement builds a culture of celebration and reinforces the commitment to achieving the ultimate goal.

To keep the shared vision alive and relevant, leaders should periodically revisit and refine the vision as needed. The business landscape may evolve, and new opportunities or challenges may arise. By adapting the vision to changing circumstances, leaders ensure that it remains a guiding force that inspires the team and aligns with the organization's long-term goals.

In conclusion, inspiring a shared vision among team members is a transformational leadership skill that fosters collaboration, commitment, and collective success. By communicating the vision authentically, involving team members in the process, and creating a culture of trust and empowerment, leaders can cultivate a shared sense of purpose that unites the team towards a common goal. This shared vision becomes the driving force that propels the organization towards greatness, achieving results that surpass individual efforts and leaving a lasting positive impact on both the team and the organization.

PART THREE:

Building a Strong Team

In the dynamic world of business, erecting a strong platoon is a critical factor that determines an association's success. A strong platoon isn't just a collection of individualities; it's a cohesive unit with a participating sense of purpose, collective trust, and reciprocal chops. Effective platoon structure leads to increased productivity, better collaboration, and a positive work culture. To make a strong platoon, leaders must concentrate on fostering open communication, nurturing a probative terrain, and icing that platoon members are aligned with the association's pretensions.

Effective communication lies at the core of erecting a strong platoon. Leaders should encourage open and transparent communication, where platoon members feel comfortable participating in ideas, enterprises, and feedback. Active listening is essential to understand the requirements and burdens of each platoon member, leading to a deeper connection and better collaboration. By promoting effective communication, leaders produce a terrain where different perspectives are valued, and innovative ideas can flourish.

Trust is the foundation upon which a strong platoon is erected. Leaders must demonstrate responsibility and be willing to trust their platoon members' capabilities. A culture of trust encourages threat- taking, fosters creativity, and empowers platoon members to take power of their work. Leaders should also encourage peer-to- peer trust, icing that platoon members support and calculate on each other to achieve common pretensions.

Nurturing a probative terrain is vital for erecting a strong platoon. Leaders should celebrate individual and platoon accomplishments, feting and appreciating the sweats of platoon members. Formative feedback should be delivered in a way that encourages growth and development, rather than causing despondency. When platoon members feel supported and valued, they're more likely to be engaged, motivated, and committed to their work.

icing that platoon members are aligned with the association's pretensions and values is pivotal for platoon structure. Leaders should easily communicate the association's vision, charge, and values, allowing platoon members to understand how their places contribute to the overall objectives. A participating sense of purpose creates a unified platoon that's concentrated on achieving common pretensions and is driven by a collaborative passion for the association's success.

Diversity in chops, backgrounds, and perspectives enriches a platoon's capabilities and problem- working capacities. Leaders should laboriously seek diversity when erecting their brigades, as it leads to further creative and well-rounded results. A different platoon fosters a culture of literacy and promotes nonstop enhancement.

In conclusion, erecting a strong platoon is a strategic imperative for organisational success. Leaders must prioritise effective communication, trust, and a probative terrain to foster platoon cohesion and productivity. By aligning platoon members with the association's pretensions and valuing diversity, leaders can cultivate a high-performing platoon that thrives on collaboration, invention, and participation success. A strong platoon becomes a driving force that propels the association towards greatness, conforming to challenges, and achieving remarkable results.

1.Recruiting the Right Talent:

A Strategic Approach to Building High-Performing Teams

In the competitive landscape of business, recruiting the right people is a crucial factor that directly impacts an organization's success. The right talent not only holds the necessary skills and qualifications but also aligns with the organization's values, culture, and long-term goals. An effective recruitment strategy ensures that the organization draws top-tier candidates, assembles high-performing teams, and cultivates a positive work environment. To acquire the right talent, organizations must focus on strategic planning, effective sourcing, streamlined selection processes, and candidate experience.

Strategic planning is the foundation of great talent recruitment. Before initiating the hiring process, organizations must outline clear job requirements, role responsibilities, and expectations. A well-defined job description not only helps candidates understand the role but also assists recruiters in finding the right talent. Additionally, organizations should conduct a thorough analysis of their current talent pool and identify skills gaps to determine the specific competencies needed for each job.

Effective sourcing is important to attract a diverse and qualified candidate group. Organizations should leverage multiple channels to reach potential candidates, including job boards, social media platforms, networking events, and employee recommendations. Engaging with passive candidates and building a talent pipeline is equally important, as it helps organisations to tap into a pool of potential candidates for future jobs.

Streamlining the selection process is vital to ensure a seamless and efficient application experience. Lengthy and cumbersome selection processes can deter top talent from pursuing opportunities with the company. By optimizing the recruitment process, organizations can engage prospects promptly, showing respect for their time and interest. Implementing pre-employment assessments and using data-driven selection techniques can help assess applicants objectively and identify the best fit for the organization.

Cultural fit is a key aspect of recruiting the right talent. Organizations should assess candidates not only based on their skills and qualifications but also on their alignment with the company's ideals and culture. A candidate who shares the organisation's vision and values is more likely to be engaged, motivated, and committed to adding to the company's long-term success.

Candidate experience plays a significant role in attracting and keeping top talent. The recruitment process should be transparent, informative, and respectful of applicants' needs. Regular communication with candidates throughout the process helps build a positive employer brand and enhances the candidate experience, regardless of the end result.

In addition to traditional qualifications, companies should assess candidates' potential for growth and adaptability. Identifying candidates who possess a growth mindset and the ability to learn and thrive in a dynamic environment is important for future-proofing the organization.

Incorporating diversity and inclusion in the recruitment process improves creativity, innovation, and decision-making. Organizations should adopt unbiased recruitment processes, strive for diverse candidate pools, and build an inclusive work environment that welcomes employees from diverse backgrounds.

Finally, ongoing evaluation and continuous improvement of the recruitment process are important to ensure its effectiveness. Collecting feedback from candidates and hiring managers allows organizations to identify areas of improvement and refine their recruitment strategy constantly.

In conclusion, recruiting the right talent is a strategic endeavor that requires careful planning, effective sourcing, streamlined processes, and a focus on candidate experience. Organizations that value cultural fit, diversity, and growth potential in addition to traditional qualifications are more likely to attract top-tier candidates who become valuable assets to the organization. By building an efficient and inclusive recruitment process, organizations can build high-performing teams that drive innovation, growth, and long-term success. A strategic approach to talent recruitment strengthens the organization's competitive advantage and positions it for success in a rapidly evolving business world.

2.Fostering a Positive and Collaborative Work Culture:

The Key to Employee Engagement and Organisational Success

A positive and collaborative work culture is the backbone of a successful company. It provides an environment where employees feel valued, motivated, and empowered to perform at their best. A culture of positivity and collaboration not only improves employee well-being but also drives innovation, productivity, and overall organizational success. To foster such a work atmosphere, businesses must prioritize open communication, recognize and celebrate achievements, promote teamwork, and invest in employee development.

Open communication is the foundation of a good work culture. Leaders and managers should encourage transparent and honest communication with workers at all levels. This includes constantly seeking feedback, addressing concerns, and being receptive to new ideas. By fostering open dialogue, employees feel heard and valued, leading to increased trust and a feeling of belonging.

Recognizing and celebrating successes is important for employee morale and motivation. Acknowledging workers' efforts, milestones, and successes cultivates a culture of appreciation and gratitude. Recognition can be given through verbal praise, public acknowledgment, or different employee recognition programs. Celebrating achievements not only boosts individual confidence but also creates a sense of collective pride among team members.

Promoting teamwork and collaboration pushes employees to work together towards shared goals. Leaders should create an environment where teamwork is valued and rewarded. Encouraging cross-functional collaboration and organizing team-building events can strengthen bonds among team members and increase their problem-solving capabilities.

Investing in employee development is important for both individual growth and organizational success. Organizations should provide chances for training, skill development, and job advancement. A culture that supports continuous learning and growth encourages employees to take ownership of their professional development, leading to increased productivity and engagement.

Emphasizing work-life balance and employee well-being is vital to a positive work culture. Organizations should offer flexible work arrangements, wellness programs, and initiatives that support work-life integration. Prioritizing employee well-being provides a supportive atmosphere that fosters employee satisfaction and reduces burnout.

Leaders play a pivotal part in shaping a positive and collaborative work culture. They should lead by example, embodying the beliefs and behaviors that they wish to see in their teams. Authentic leadership and a focus on employee development promote trust and inspire employees to take initiative and contribute to the organization's success.

In conclusion, creating a positive and collaborative work culture is a strategic approach that reaps significant benefits for both workers and organizations. An environment of open communication, recognition, teamwork, and employee growth improves employee engagement, satisfaction, and productivity. Such a work culture attracts and retains top talent, supports innovation, and positions the company for long-term success in a competitive business landscape. By prioritizing a positive work culture, organizations create a thriving and motivated workforce that drives greatness and pushes the organization towards its goals.

PART FOUR .

Developing a Solid Business Plan:

The Roadmap to Success

A solid business plan is the blueprint that leads entrepreneurs and organizations towards success. It acts as a comprehensive document that outlines the vision, purpose, strategies, and financial projections of a business venture. Developing a robust business plan requires careful analysis, strategic thinking, and a clear understanding of the market and industry environment. A well-crafted business plan not only helps gain funding from investors but also provides a roadmap for sustainable growth and effective decision-making. To build a solid business plan, entrepreneurs must focus on key aspects such as market analysis, competitive positioning, operational strategies, financial projections, and risk assessment.

Market analysis is a critical component of a good business plan. Entrepreneurs must perform thorough research to understand the target market, customer needs, and industry trends. Market analysis includes studying customer demographics, preferences, and buying behavior, as well as evaluating the size of the market and its growth potential. This data helps entrepreneurs spot opportunities, assess market demand, and position their products or services successfully.

Competitive positioning includes understanding the strengths and weaknesses of competitors and how the business will differentiate itself in the market. Analyzing competitors' products, pricing strategies, marketing efforts, and market share helps entrepreneurs find gaps in the market and create unique selling propositions. A clear knowledge of competitive positioning ensures that the business can effectively target its ideal customers and gain a competitive advantage.

Operational strategies outline how the business will offer its products or services and handle its day-to-day operations. This includes establishing the necessary resources, production methods, distribution channels, and logistics. Defining operational strategies ensures that the business can efficiently offer value to customers while managing costs and resources effectively.

Financial projections are a critical aspect of a solid business plan, giving a realistic assessment of the financial viability of the venture. This includes projecting revenue, expenses, and cash flow over a specific period, usually three to five years. Financial projections help investors and stakeholders understand the possible return on investment and the sustainability of the business over time.

Risk assessment includes identifying potential challenges and risks that the business may face. These may include market volatility, legal changes, operational disruptions, or financial limits. By anticipating and addressing risks proactively, entrepreneurs can create contingency plans and mitigate possible challenges, ensuring the long-term viability of the business.

A well-structured business plan should also include a thorough marketing and sales strategy. This outlines how the business will attract and retain customers, promote its goods or services, and achieve its sales targets. The marketing and sales strategy should align with the market research and competitive positioning to ensure successful customer acquisition and brand recognition.

Furthermore, a solid business plan should outline the organizational framework and management team. Investors and stakeholders are interested in knowing the key people responsible for executing the business plan and their qualifications and experience. Highlighting the strengths of the management team helps build trust in the business's ability to succeed.

In conclusion, developing a solid business plan is a critical step for any entrepreneur or organization starting on a new venture. A well-crafted business plan provides a clear roadmap for success, leading the business towards its goals and objectives. By conducting comprehensive market analysis, defining competitive positioning, outlining operational strategies, projecting financials, and assessing risks, entrepreneurs can create a comprehensive and persuasive business plan that instills confidence in investors and sets the foundation for sustainable growth and success. A solid business plan serves as a powerful tool for decision-making, resource allocation, and achieving long-term profitability in the ever-changing business environment.

1.Creating a Roadmap for Success:

Charting the Path to Achievement

A roadmap for success is a strategic plan that outlines the steps and milestones necessary to achieve particular goals and objectives. Whether in business, personal development, or any other endeavor, creating a roadmap offers clarity, direction, and focus. It serves as a guiding framework, helping people and organizations manage challenges, make informed decisions, and stay on track towards achieving their desired outcomes. To create an effective roadmap for success, one must set clear goals, establish actionable steps, prioritize tasks, assign resources wisely, and be adaptable to changes along the way.

Setting clear and specific goals is the basis of a successful roadmap. Goals should be realistic, measurable, and time-bound, giving a clear vision of what success looks like. Whether it's increasing revenue by a certain percentage, launching a new product, or meeting personal growth milestones, well-defined goals serve as the driving force behind the roadmap.

Once the goals are set, the next step is to break them down into actionable steps. These steps reflect the specific tasks and actions that need to be taken to progress towards the goals. Each step should be clear, achievable, and aligned with the overall goal. Breaking the goals into smaller, manageable tasks makes the journey to success less overwhelming and allows steady progress.

Prioritization is important in creating a roadmap for success. Not all jobs are of equal importance or urgency. Identifying the important tasks that have a significant impact on achieving the goals is crucial for effective time and resource management. Prioritizing tasks helps individuals and organizations stay focused on what matters most and avoid getting sidetracked by less important activities.

Allocating resources wisely is another key aspect of a good roadmap. Resources include not only cash assets but also time, skills, and manpower. Careful resource allocation ensures that there are enough resources available to support the roadmap's completion. It includes identifying potential constraints and planning for contingencies to ensure smooth progress towards the goals.

Flexibility and adaptability are vital to a successful roadmap. The journey to success is often filled with unforeseen challenges and changes in the external world. A roadmap that allows for adjustments and course corrections enables people and organizations to react proactively to changing circumstances and remain resilient in the face of adversity.

Regular monitoring and review are important to the success of a roadmap. Progress towards the goals should be tracked regularly, and accomplishments should be celebrated. Concurrently, any deviations from the plan should be analyzed, and tweaks should be made to realign the roadmap with the desired results.

Moreover, involving key stakeholders and team members in the roadmap creation process promotes a sense of ownership and accountability. Collaborative input and feedback ensure that diverse views are considered, resulting in a more comprehensive and well-rounded roadmap. Team alignment with the roadmap's vision and goals improves motivation, commitment, and collaboration.

In conclusion, creating a roadmap for success is an important step in achieving goals and objectives, whether in business, personal growth, or any other pursuit. A well-crafted roadmap provides direction, clarity, and focus, guiding people and organizations towards their desired outcomes. By setting clear goals, establishing actionable steps, prioritizing tasks, allocating resources wisely, and being adaptable to changes, individuals and organizations can create a powerful roadmap that empowers them to overcome challenges and take opportunities along the journey to success. With a roadmap in hand, individuals and organizations can surely follow their aspirations, overcome obstacles, and achieve remarkable results.

2.Financial Projections and Resource Allocation:

The Bedrock of Strategic Planning

Financial projections and resource allocation are two interconnected components that form the bedrock of strategic planning for people and organizations alike. Financial projections involve forecasting future financial performance, while resource allocation refers to the efficient spread of assets, including financial resources, human capital, and time, to achieve specific goals and objectives. By integrating these aspects into the strategic planning process, individuals and organizations can make informed decisions, improve performance, and effectively achieve their desired outcomes.

Financial projections are important for planning and decision-making, providing a glimpse into the financial health and sustainability of a project, business, or initiative. Forecasting revenues, expenses, cash flow, and profitability over a specific time helps people and organizations assess their financial viability and potential return on investment. Financial projections enable better decision-making by providing insights into the financial impact of different strategies, scenarios, and potential risks.

To create accurate financial projections, individuals and organizations must conduct thorough market analysis, evaluate historical financial data, and consider economic trends and industry benchmarks. By understanding market dynamics and competitive positioning, one can make accurate revenue forecasts. Similarly, analyzing past financial success and identifying trends allows for more accurate expense forecasting. Financial projections should be updated regularly to reflect changes in the market or business environment and to ensure they stay relevant and reliable.

Resource allocation complements financial projections by ensuring that the necessary resources are available to execute the strategic plan successfully. Efficient resource allocation involves finding the critical resources needed, prioritizing their allocation based on their importance to the overall strategy, and optimizing their use to achieve the desired outcomes.

Financial resources are one of the main components of resource allocation. Adequate funding is important to support the implementation of strategic initiatives. By aligning financial projections with resource allocation, people and organizations can ensure they have sufficient funds to execute their plans and that resources are allocated to the most critical areas of the strategy.

Human capital is another important resource that requires careful allocation. Identifying the skills and expertise needed to execute the strategic plan helps in recruiting and retaining the right people. Properly aligning employees' skills with strategic goals ensures that the company has the right people in the right roles to drive success.

Time is a finite resource that must be handled effectively. Developing a timeline for implementing the strategic plan and setting milestones helps people and organizations stay on track and watch progress. Resource allocation should consider the time needed to complete various tasks and ensure that deadlines are reasonable and achievable.

Effective resource allocation includes evaluating the opportunity cost of different options. It may require making trade-offs and prioritizing certain projects over others. By considering the potential benefits and drawbacks of different resource allocation scenarios, individuals and organizations can make informed choices that maximize value and align with their strategic objectives.

Moreover, continuous monitoring and evaluation of financial performance and resource allocation are important for course correction and optimization. Regularly comparing actual results with financial projections and resource allocation plans helps individuals and organizations to spot variances and take corrective actions promptly. This iterative process of learning and adaptation improves the effectiveness of the strategic plan and increases the chance of achieving the desired outcomes.

In conclusion, financial projections and resource allocation are integral components of strategic planning, providing the basis for informed decision-making and effective goal attainment. Financial projections offer insights into the financial health and sustainability of a project, business, or venture. Resource allocation ensures that the necessary financial, human, and time resources are efficiently distributed to achieve strategic goals. By integrating financial projections with resource allocation, individuals and organizations can improve performance, manage risks, and align their efforts with their desired outcomes. A well-crafted strategic plan that integrates financial projections and resource allocation sets the road for success, helping people and organizations navigate challenges, seize opportunities, and achieve their goals in an ever-changing business landscape.

PART FIVE .

Effective Product Development:

From Ideation to Market Success

Effective product development is a strategic and dynamic process that closes the gap between innovation and market success. It involves transforming ideas and concepts into tangible products that meet customer needs and generate value for the company. A well-executed product creation method not only drives innovation but also minimizes risks, maximizes resource utilization, and accelerates time to market. To achieve successful product development, organizations must value customer-centricity, rigorous market research, agile methodologies, cross-functional collaboration, and continuous iteration and improvement.

Customer-centricity is the foundation of effective product creation. Understanding customer wants, pain points, and preferences is important for creating products that resonate with the target market. Engaging with customers through surveys, interviews, and user testing provides valuable insights that guide product design and development. By placing the customer at the center of the process, organizations can ensure that their goods are relevant, valuable, and market-driven.

Rigorous market study is a crucial step in effective product development. Analyzing market trends, competitor offerings, and customer behavior helps companies find gaps and opportunities. Market research informs product positioning, pricing, and marketing strategies, allowing organizations to make informed decisions that increase the product's chances of success in the market.

Agile methods have become increasingly popular in product development due to their flexibility and adaptability. Adopting agile practices helps organizations to react quickly to changing customer needs and market dynamics. The iterative nature of agile development allows continuous feedback and improvement, reducing the risk of investing resources in goods that do not meet market demands.

Cross-functional collaboration is important for effective product development. Bringing together diverse skills from product management, design, engineering, marketing, and other relevant areas fosters a holistic approach to product development. Collaborative teams can better handle complex challenges, streamline decision-making, and ensure that all aspects of the product are aligned with the overall goal.

Continuous iteration and improvement are integral to successful product development. Launching an initial version of the product, gathering user feedback, and making iterative changes based on that feedback allows organizations to refine the product to better meet customer needs. This iterative process, often referred to as the Minimum Viable Product (MVP) method, reduces the risk of developing a product that does not connect with the market and maximizes the return on investment.

Moreover, effective product development needs a clear understanding of the product's value proposition. Defining the unique selling points and the value that the product brings to customers helps organizations differentiate their goods in a crowded market. The value proposition guides product development choices and messaging, ensuring that the product meets customer needs and stands out from the competition.

In addition to the development phase, successful product development includes a well-thought-out product launch and go-to-market strategy. A successful launch includes coordinated marketing efforts, sales enablement, and customer support to build awareness and drive adoption. A robust go-to-market strategy ensures that the product gets the right audience through the most effective channels.

Continuous monitoring and feedback collection after the product launch are crucial for assessing the product's success and making necessary adjustments. Organizations should measure key performance indicators (KPIs) and gather customer comments to evaluate the product's success in the market. This data-driven method enables organizations to identify areas for improvement and refine their product development and marketing strategies.

In conclusion, successful product development is a multifaceted and customer-centric process that brings innovation to life and drives market success. It involves rigorous market research, agile methodologies, cross-functional teamwork, and continuous iteration to create products that meet customer needs and provide value. By adopting a data-driven approach and staying responsive to market feedback, organizations can develop products that connect with customers, maximize return on investment, and establish a competitive advantage. Effective product development is a strategic imperative for organizations seeking sustained growth and success in a dynamic and competitive business environment.

1.Design Thinking and Product Validation:

Building Customer-Centric Solutions

Design thought and product validation are two interrelated processes that play a pivotal role in building successful and customer-centric solutions. Design thinking is a human-centered method to problem-solving that focuses on understanding user needs, ideating creative solutions, prototyping, and iterating based on user feedback. Product validation, on the other hand, includes testing and gathering feedback from potential users to ensure that the proposed product or solution addresses their pain points and meets their expectations. By integrating design thinking and product validation into the product development process, organizations can build products that resonate with customers, reduce the risk of failure, and increase the chance of market success.

Design thinking starts with empathizing with the end-users to understand their goals, motivations, and pain points. This includes conducting interviews, observations, and surveys to gain deep insights into users' experiences and challenges. By empathizing with users, product teams can identify unmet needs and opportunities, setting the foundation for innovative and customer-centric solutions.

Once user needs are understood, the ideation phase starts. In this step, cross-functional teams brainstorm and generate a wide range of ideas to address the identified needs. The focus is on quantity and diversity of ideas, supporting creativity and thinking beyond conventional answers. This divergent thinking process allows teams to explore various possibilities and create novel ways to solving user problems.

The next step is to prototype the most interesting ideas. Prototypes are tangible representations of the proposed solutions that allow users to interact with and provide feedback on the ideas. Prototyping allows organisations to validate ideas quickly and cost-effectively before investing resources in full-scale development. This iterative approach saves time and resources, as it allows teams to learn from user feedback and improve the solutions based on real-world insights.

Product validation is an important aspect of the design thinking process. It includes gathering feedback from potential users to assess the desirability, usability, and viability of the suggested product or solution. Validation can take various forms, such as polls, focus groups, usability testing, or early product trials. By validating the product with the target audience, organisations ensure that they are building something that truly meets user needs and aligns with user expectations.

User feedback obtained during product validation is invaluable for refining the product and making informed choices. It helps teams spot potential issues and opportunities for improvement early in the development process. By listening to user feedback, product teams can pivot, adapt, and iterate to build solutions that are more likely to succeed in the market.

Design thought and product validation are not linear processes; they are iterative and continuous. As the product evolves, so does the knowledge of user needs and market dynamics. Product teams must be open to embracing new insights and making changes based on ongoing feedback and changing requirements.

Moreover, customer involvement is key to both design thinking and product validation. Engaging customers throughout the development process promotes a sense of ownership and ensures that the final product meets their expectations. Customer co-creation and collaboration lead to better user satisfaction, increased adoption, and brand loyalty.

In conclusion, design thinking and product validation are powerful tools for building customer-centric solutions that resonate with users and increase the chance of market success. By empathising with users, ideating creative solutions, prototyping, and validating ideas with the target audience, organisations can create products that truly meet customer needs and expectations. These iterative and human-centred approaches allow teams to learn from user feedback, refine the solutions, and make informed decisions to offer high-quality products. Embracing design thought and product validation as integral parts of the product development process empowers organisations to create innovative and customer-centric solutions that drive business growth and competitiveness in a rapidly changing marketplace.

2.Iterative Development and Continuous Improvement:

The Path to Excellence

Iterative development and continuous improvement are two important principles that drive excellence in project management, and organisational success. These methods embracental progress and learning. By adopting iterative development and fostering a culture of continuous improvement, organisations can enhance product quality, optimise processes, and stay responsive to evolving customer wants and market dynamics.

Iterative development is a methodology that breaks down complex projects or goods into smaller, manageable iterations. Instead of trying to achieve perfection in a single large release, iterative development focuses on providing incremental improvements through multiple cycles. Each iteration builds on the lessons learned from earlier ones, allowing teams to refine the product, adapt to changing requirements, and incorporate user feedback in real-time.

The benefits of iterative growth are manifold. First and foremost, it reduces the chance of costly and time-consuming failures. By providing smaller, functional components at regular intervals, organisations can identify and address issues early in the development process, minimising the impact of potential defects or changes in requirements.

Moreover, iterative development allows rapid delivery and time-to-market. Instead of waiting for a complete product, customers can start benefiting from the delivered features as soon as each iteration is finished. This fosters a closer relationship between the development team and the end-users, leading to greater user satisfaction and improved trust in the product.

Iterative development also supports a culture of collaboration and learning within the company. Cross-functional teams work together to deliver each iteration, supporting collective ownership and accountability. The iterative process allows teams to gather insights from user feedback, test theories, and continuously improve the product based on real-world insights.

Continuous improvement complements iterative development by stressing the ongoing refinement and optimization of processes, practices, and products. It is a mindset that challenges the status quo and tries to make incremental and sustained improvements in every part of the organisation's operations.

The principles of continuous improvement can be traced back to the Japanese concept of Kaizen, which promotes a culture of continuous small changes. In a business context, this approach involves encouraging employees at all levels to spot inefficiencies, propose ideas for improvement, and implement changes that lead to increased productivity, quality, and customer satisfaction.

Continuous improvement is driven by a dedication to data-driven decision-making. Organisations collect and analyse data to find areas for improvement, measure success, and make informed choices. Key performance indicators (KPIs) and metrics are used to track performance and measure the effect of changes.

To promote a culture of continuous improvement, organisations must provide employees with the tools, resources, and support needed to contribute actively to the process. Encouraging open communication and creating a safe place for sharing ideas and feedback empowers employees to take ownership of their work and seek ways to improve performance.

Furthermore, continuous improvement is not limited to individual processes or projects; it extends to company culture and leadership practices. Leaders must set the tone for continuous improvement by being receptive to new ideas, encouraging experimentation, and recognizing and celebrating successes.

In conclusion, iterative development and continuous improvement are strong drivers of excellence and success in today's dynamic and competitive business environment. Embracing iterative development allows organisations to deliver products faster, react to customer feedback more effectively, and reduce the risk of failure. Continuous improvement, as a cultural mindset, enables organisations to optimise processes, enhance performance, and promote a culture of innovation and excellence. By integrating these concepts into their operations, organisations can achieve excellence, stay relevant in a changing market, and create lasting value for their customers and stakeholders.

PART SIX

Marketing and Branding Strategies.

Marketing and branding strategies are integral components of a successful business that aim to build brand awareness, attract customers, and establish a unique identity in the marketplace. While marketing focuses on promoting products or services, branding is about creating a distinctive personality and emotional connection with the target audience. By developing effective marketing and branding strategies, organisations can differentiate themselves from competitors, cultivate customer loyalty, and drive sustainable growth.

1. Defining the Target Audience: The first step in developing marketing and branding strategies is to define the target audience. Understanding the demographics, preferences, and pain points of the target market helps organisations tailor their messaging and positioning to resonate with potential customers. This customer-centric approach ensures that marketing efforts reach the right audience and elicit a positive response.

2. Brand Identity and Positioning: Branding strategies revolve around creating a strong brand identity and positioning. This involves defining the brand's mission, values, personality, and unique selling proposition (USP). A clear and compelling brand identity helps customers connect with the brand on a deeper level and creates a distinct image in their minds.

3. Consistent Brand Messaging: Consistency in brand messaging across all marketing channels

is crucial for reinforcing brand identity and building brand recognition. Whether it's through advertising, social media, or customer interactions, maintaining a consistent tone, voice, and visual elements helps establish brand credibility and trust.

4. Omni-Channel Marketing: Effective marketing strategies utilise multiple channels to reach the target audience. From traditional advertising to digital marketing, a well-rounded omni-channel approach maximises the brand's exposure and engages customers at different touchpoints. This seamless integration across channels ensures a cohesive brand experience for customers.

5. Content Marketing: Content marketing plays a vital role in educating and engaging customers. By creating valuable, relevant, and informative content, organisations can position themselves as industry experts and build trust with their audience. Content marketing also supports

search engine optimization (SEO) efforts, driving organic traffic to the brand's website.

6. Social Media Engagement: Social media has become a powerful tool for marketing and branding. Engaging with customers on social platforms allows organisations to listen to feedback, respond to queries, and humanise the brand. Social media also facilitates word-of-mouth marketing as satisfied customers share their experiences with others.

7. Influencer Marketing: Collaborating with influencers who align with the brand's values and target audience can amplify the brand's reach and credibility. Influencers have a strong influence on their followers, and their endorsements can drive brand awareness and product adoption.

8. Customer Relationship Management (CRM): Building strong customer relationships is essential for customer retention and loyalty. Utilising CRM tools helps organisations track

customer interactions, personalise communication, and provide exceptional customer service.

9. Data-Driven Marketing: Data analytics and market research play a vital role in refining marketing strategies. Analysing customer behaviour, market trends, and campaign performance helps organisations make data-driven decisions and optimise their marketing efforts.

10. Measuring and Evaluating Results: Monitoring key performance indicators (KPIs) and evaluating the success of marketing and branding strategies are critical for continuous improvement. Measuring ROI, conversion rates, customer acquisition costs, and customer satisfaction helps organisations identify areas for optimization and refine their strategies accordingly.

In conclusion, effective marketing and branding strategies are essential for building brand awareness, engaging customers, and driving business growth. Defining the target audience, establishing a strong brand identity, and maintaining consistent messaging are fundamental steps in branding. Implementing omni-channel marketing, content marketing, social media engagement, and influencer marketing expands the brand's reach and credibility. Utilising data-driven insights and continuously evaluating performance helps organisations refine their strategies and stay responsive to market dynamics. By integrating these strategies into their operations, organisations can create a compelling brand presence, foster customer loyalty, and achieve long-term success in a competitive marketplace.

1.Identifying Target Customers and Segments:

Unleashing the Power of Precision Marketing

In the dynamic and competitive landscape of modern business, the key to a successful marketing plan lies in identifying target customers and segments. This process includes understanding the unique needs, preferences, and behaviours of the ideal crowd to create personalised and engaging marketing campaigns. By segmenting the market, companies can group customers with similar characteristics, allowing them to tailor their messaging and offerings to each specific segment. This precision marketing method optimises resources, improves customer satisfaction, and yields higher returns on marketing investments.

1. Market Research and Analysis: The journey of identifying target customers and segments starts with comprehensive market research and analysis. Gathering data on market size, demographics, psychographics, buying behaviours, and preferences of possible customers is important. By using surveys, focus groups, and data analytics, companies can gain valuable insights into the needs and pain points of their audience.

2. Define Ideal Customer Profiles: Based on the market research, companies can create detailed customer profiles that represent their ideal customers. These profiles typically include information such as age, gender, location, income level, hobbies, lifestyle, and purchase behaviour. Defining ideal customer profiles helps businesses better understand their target

group and tailor marketing messages accordingly.

3. Segmentation Strategies: Segmentation includes dividing the target market into distinct groups or segments based on shared characteristics. Common segmentation techniques include demographic, geographic, psychographic, and behavioural segmentation. Demographic segmentation separates the market based on age, gender, income, and other demographic factors. Geographic segmentation categorises people based on their location. Psychographic segmentation includes customers' lifestyle, values, and interests. Behavioural segmentation groups customers based on their purchasing behaviour and company interactions.

4. Benefit and Need Segmentation: Another valuable segmentation technique is benefit and need segmentation. This method groups customers based on the specific benefits they seek from a product or service or the needs they want to fulfil. By knowing the specific

motivations of different customer segments, businesses can create targeted marketing messages that resonate with each group.

5. Customer Journey Mapping: Mapping the customer journey is a crucial step in finding target customers and segments. It includes understanding the various touchpoints and interactions customers have with the brand throughout their decision-making process. Customer journey mapping helps businesses spot pain points, opportunities for engagement, and areas where marketing efforts can be optimised.

6. Personalization and Customization: Armed with insights from market research and segmentation, businesses can tailor their marketing campaigns to deliver personalised and customised messages to each target group. Personalization enhances customer experience and creates a deeper emotional connection with the brand, boosting customer loyalty and retention.

7. Test and Iterate: Identifying target customers and segments is an ongoing process that needs constant monitoring and iteration. Businesses should constantly gather customer feedback, measure the performance of marketing campaigns, and adapt their strategies accordingly. Testing different messages, platforms, and offers allows organisations to refine their approach and identify what connects most with their target audience.

8. Customer Data and Technology: Leveraging customer data and technology is important for identifying and reaching target customers and segments. Customer relationship management (CRM) systems, data analytics tools, and marketing automation platforms help businesses collect and analyse customer data, segment their audience successfully, and execute precision marketing campaigns.

In conclusion, finding target customers and segments is a strategic process that allows businesses to connect with their audience on a deeper level and deliver personalised marketing experiences. Through market research, customer profiling, and segmentation strategies, businesses gain valuable insights into customer needs, behaviours, and preferences. Precision marketing allows businesses to optimise their resources, improve customer engagement, and increase the efficiency of their marketing efforts. By embracing precision marketing and continually refining their approach based on customer insights, organisations can promote brand loyalty, achieve higher conversion rates, and thrive in a competitive marketplace.

2. Building Brand Identity and Market Positioning:

Crafting a Memorable and Relevant Brand Image

Brand identity and market positioning are essential elements of a successful marketing strategy that shape how a brand is perceived by its target audience. Brand identity encompasses the unique characteristics, values, and personality that define a brand, while market positioning involves the deliberate effort to differentiate the brand from competitors and occupy a distinct and favourable space in the minds of consumers. By effectively building brand identity and market positioning, businesses can create a memorable and relevant brand image that resonates with customers and sets them apart in a competitive marketplace.

1. Define the Brand Identity: The first step in building a brand identity is to define the brand's purpose, values, and personality. This involves answering questions such as "What does the brand stand for?" "What are its core values?" and "What personality traits does the brand exhibit?" A clear and authentic brand identity provides the foundation for all brand-related activities and ensures consistency across marketing efforts.

2. Craft a Compelling Brand Story: Storytelling is a powerful tool in building brand identity. By creating a compelling brand story that evokes emotions and connects with customers on a deeper level, businesses can establish an emotional bond with their audience. A well-crafted brand story communicates the brand's mission, values, and unique selling

proposition in a way that captures the hearts and minds of consumers.

3. Design the Visual Identity: The visual identity of a brand is the visual representation of its personality and values. This includes elements such as the logo, colour palette, typography, and brand imagery. A well-designed visual identity reinforces the brand's message and helps create a consistent and recognizable brand image across all marketing channels.

4. Consistent Brand Messaging: Building a strong brand identity requires consistency in messaging. Whether in advertising, social media, or customer communications, the brand's tone, voice, and messaging should align with its identity. Consistent messaging enhances brand recognition and builds trust with customers.

5. Understand the Target Audience: Market positioning begins with a deep understanding of the target audience. Analysing customer demographics, preferences, and behaviours helps

businesses identify what sets their target audience apart and what unique needs or desires they have. This understanding enables businesses to tailor their positioning to resonate with the specific needs and aspirations of their customers.

6. Identify the Unique Selling Proposition (USP): A strong market positioning is based on a clear and compelling unique selling proposition (USP). The USP defines what makes the brand stand out and why customers should choose it over competitors. It highlights the brand's competitive advantage and addresses the specific pain points or desires of the target audience.

7. Competitor Analysis: Understanding the competitive landscape is crucial for effective market positioning. Analysing competitors' strengths and weaknesses helps businesses identify gaps in the market and opportunities to differentiate their brand. Market positioning should focus on areas where the brand can excel and deliver superior value to customers.

8. Communicate the Value Proposition: Communicating the brand's value proposition is essential for market positioning. Whether through advertising, content marketing, or product packaging, businesses should clearly communicate how their brand addresses the needs of their target audience and delivers unique benefits.

9. Deliver on Promises: Market positioning is not just about communicating a message; it is also about delivering on promises. Consistently meeting or exceeding customer expectations builds brand trust and loyalty. A strong market positioning can only be sustained if the brand consistently delivers on its brand promise.

10. Monitor and Adapt: Market positioning is an ongoing process that requires continuous monitoring and adaptation. Customer preferences and market dynamics evolve, and successful brands remain agile in adjusting their

positioning strategies to stay relevant and competitive.

In conclusion, building brand identity and market positioning are critical elements of a successful marketing strategy that enables businesses to create a memorable and relevant brand image. A well-defined brand identity that communicates the brand's purpose, values, and personality lays the foundation for all marketing efforts. Market positioning involves understanding the target audience, identifying the unique selling proposition, and differentiating the brand from competitors. By crafting a compelling brand story, designing a visually appealing brand identity, and delivering on promises, businesses can establish a strong brand presence that resonates with customers and sets them apart in a competitive marketplace. Continuous monitoring and adaptation ensure that the brand remains relevant and maintains a favourable position in the minds of consumers.

PART SEVEN.

Navigating Funding and Finance:

Strategies for Securing Capital and Managing Finances

For businesses, navigating funding and finance is a critical aspect of sustaining and growing their operations. Whether starting a new venture or expanding an existing one, securing capital and effectively managing finances are essential to ensure stability and success. This process involves exploring various funding options, creating a financial plan, and adopting sound financial management practices. By understanding the landscape of funding and finance, businesses can make informed decisions to support their growth and achieve their long-term objectives.

1. Funding Options:
- Self-Funding (Bootstrapping): Entrepreneurs can use personal savings, credit cards, or loans from family and friends to self-fund their businesses. Bootstrapping allows full control and avoids equity dilution, but it may have limitations in terms of the amount of capital available.
- Equity Financing: In exchange for capital, businesses can sell ownership shares (equity) to investors, such as angel investors or venture capitalists. Equity financing provides access to substantial funding, but it may involve giving up partial ownership and decision-making control.
- Debt Financing: Borrowing money through loans or lines of credit from banks, financial institutions, or private lenders is a common form

of debt financing. Businesses must repay the principal amount with interest, but they retain full ownership and control over their operations.

- Crowdfunding: Utilising online platforms, businesses can raise funds from a large number of individual investors who contribute smaller amounts. Crowdfunding can generate awareness and customer engagement in addition to funding.

- Government Grants and Subsidies: Governments often offer grants and subsidies to support specific industries or projects. These sources of funding can be competitive but can provide financial support without equity dilution.

2. Financial Planning:

- Budgeting: Creating a comprehensive budget helps businesses allocate resources efficiently and set financial targets. Budgets should include income projections, expense estimates, and contingency plans.

- Cash Flow Management: Monitoring cash flow is crucial for ensuring liquidity and meeting financial obligations. Businesses should

carefully manage receivables, payables, and working capital to maintain a healthy cash flow.
- Financial Projections: Building realistic financial projections based on market research and historical data helps businesses anticipate future revenue and expenses. Projections assist in making informed decisions and securing funding from investors and lenders.

3. Financial Management:
- Accounting and Bookkeeping: Maintaining accurate and up-to-date financial records is essential for compliance, reporting, and decision-making. Businesses should implement effective accounting and bookkeeping practices to track financial transactions and performance.
- Risk Management: Identifying and managing financial risks is critical for business sustainability. Businesses should assess potential risks such as economic fluctuations, changes in consumer behaviour, or industry-specific risks and develop risk mitigation strategies.
- Cost Control: Prudent cost control measures help businesses optimise their spending and

improve profitability. Regularly reviewing expenses and identifying areas for cost reduction or efficiency gains can contribute to financial health.

4. Building and Maintaining Relationships:
- Investors and Lenders: Businesses should cultivate relationships with potential investors and lenders, focusing on transparent communication and building trust. Maintaining open lines of communication can lead to ongoing support and opportunities for future funding.
- Financial Advisors and Consultants: Seeking guidance from financial advisors or consultants can provide businesses with valuable insights and expertise in making financial decisions, managing risk, and optimising financial strategies.

In conclusion, navigating funding and finance requires a well-thought-out approach, including exploring various funding options, creating a financial plan, and adopting sound financial management practices. By carefully evaluating funding sources, planning for financial needs, and maintaining transparent and healthy financial practices, businesses can position themselves for success, sustainability, and growth in a dynamic and competitive business environment. Building strong relationships with investors, lenders, and financial advisors further supports businesses in achieving their financial objectives and realising their long-term vision.

1. Bootstrapping vs. seeking investors

Bootstrapping and seeking investors are two distinct approaches to funding a business, each with its advantages and considerations. Bootstrapping refers to self-funding a business using personal savings, revenue generated by the business, or contributions from friends and family. On the other hand, seeking investors involves raising capital from external sources, such as venture capitalists, angel investors, or crowdfunding platforms. Both methods have their merits and depend on the business's stage, growth objectives, and risk appetite.

Bootstrapping offers several benefits, particularly for entrepreneurs who prefer maintaining control over their business and avoiding debt or equity dilution. By self-funding the business, founders can retain full ownership and decision-making power. This level of control can be advantageous in pursuing long-term vision and maintaining the integrity of the company's mission and values.

Bootstrapping can also foster resourcefulness and financial discipline. With limited resources, entrepreneurs are encouraged to be frugal and prioritise essential expenses. This approach often leads to creative problem-solving and a lean operational structure, which can be beneficial in building a sustainable and efficient business.

Moreover, bootstrapping allows entrepreneurs to prove the business concept and validate the market demand before seeking external funding. By demonstrating early traction and revenue generation, entrepreneurs increase their chances of securing favorable investment terms when they decide to seek external funding in the future.

However, bootstrapping has its challenges. Relying solely on personal savings or limited funds may restrict the business's growth potential, as there might be limitations on hiring, marketing, and expanding to new markets. Additionally, bootstrapped businesses might face challenges in scaling quickly to meet market demands, especially in highly competitive industries.

On the other hand, seeking investors can provide businesses with a significant injection of capital to fuel rapid growth and expansion. Investors, particularly venture capitalists and angel investors, bring not only financial resources but also valuable expertise, industry connections, and strategic guidance. This external support can accelerate the business's growth trajectory and increase its chances of success.

Furthermore, external funding allows entrepreneurs to take more significant risks and pursue ambitious opportunities that might have been unattainable through bootstrapping. This capital infusion can be critical in developing new products, expanding into new markets, or acquiring competitors.

Seeking investors can also provide a level of validation and credibility to the business. The involvement of reputable investors can attract more customers, partners, and employees, enhancing the company's overall reputation and positioning in the market.

However, seeking investors also comes with trade-offs. Entrepreneurs may need to relinquish partial ownership and control of the business to accommodate the investors' interests and decision-making influence. This may lead to potential conflicts regarding strategic direction and business priorities.

Additionally, raising external funding involves the complexity of negotiating terms, conducting due diligence, and meeting investor expectations. Entrepreneurs must be prepared to demonstrate a compelling business case, robust growth potential, and a clear plan for achieving profitability and returns on investment.

In conclusion, bootstrapping and seeking investors are two viable funding options for entrepreneurs, each with its advantages and considerations. Bootstrapping allows entrepreneurs to maintain full ownership and control over the business while fostering financial discipline and creativity. Seeking investors, on the other hand, provides access to significant capital, expertise, and industry connections, enabling rapid growth and expansion. The choice between bootstrapping and seeking investors depends on the entrepreneur's objectives, risk tolerance, and growth strategy. Some businesses may opt for bootstrapping in the early stages to validate the concept, while others may seek external funding to accelerate growth and capture market opportunities. Ultimately, both approaches can lead to business success, and the key is to select the funding strategy that aligns best with the business's unique needs and vision.

2.Managing Finances and Securing Funding:

Key Practices for Business Success

Effective financial management and securing funding are essential pillars of business success. Managing finances involves maintaining a healthy cash flow, making strategic financial decisions, and optimising resources to support business operations and growth. On the other hand, securing funding is a critical step for startups and established businesses alike, as it provides the necessary capital to fuel expansion, innovation, and strategic initiatives. By combining prudent financial management practices with a well-thought-out funding strategy, businesses can achieve financial stability and position themselves for sustainable growth.

Managing Finances:

1. Budgeting and Forecasting: Creating a detailed budget and financial forecast is the foundation of effective financial management. Businesses should estimate both their revenue and expenses, considering all operational costs, variable expenses, and projected income. Budgeting helps in allocating resources wisely and avoiding overspending.

2. Cash Flow Management: Managing cash flow is crucial for business sustainability. Businesses must ensure that cash inflows exceed cash outflows, maintaining sufficient liquidity to cover day-to-day operations, payables, and unexpected expenses. Regularly reviewing cash flow and identifying potential cash flow gaps helps in proactive decision-making.

3. Cost Control: Cost control measures are essential for optimising expenses and improving profitability. Identifying non-essential or inefficient expenses and seeking cost-saving opportunities without compromising quality is vital. Businesses should continuously evaluate their cost structure to stay competitive and financially resilient.

4. Financial Analysis: Conducting regular financial analysis helps businesses gain insights into their financial health and performance. Key financial ratios and performance metrics provide valuable information about profitability, efficiency, and liquidity. Analysing financial data enables businesses to make data-driven decisions and identify areas for improvement.

5. Working Capital Management: Efficiently managing working capital, which includes accounts receivable, accounts payable, and inventory, is critical for cash flow optimization. Reducing the cash conversion cycle and ensuring timely collections and payments

contribute to better working capital management.

6. Debt Management: For businesses with debt, managing debt effectively is essential to avoid excessive interest costs and maintain a healthy balance between debt and equity. Developing a debt repayment plan and considering refinancing options can help businesses manage their debt burden.

Securing Funding:

1. Business Plan: A well-structured and comprehensive business plan is crucial for attracting potential investors and lenders. The business plan should outline the company's mission, market analysis, competitive advantage, financial projections, and funding needs.

2. Targeting the Right Investors: Identifying the right investors who align with the business's industry, stage, and growth trajectory is vital. Different investors have different investment

preferences and criteria. Startups may target angel investors and venture capitalists, while established businesses may seek private equity or institutional investors.

3. Pitching and Communication: Effectively communicating the business's value proposition and growth potential is key to securing funding. Entrepreneurs should craft a compelling pitch and confidently present their business to potential investors, emphasising how the investment will create value.

4. Networking and Relationships: Building relationships with potential investors and industry peers is an essential part of the funding process. Attending networking events, industry conferences, and startup incubators can help entrepreneurs connect with potential investors and gain valuable insights.

5. Alternative Funding Sources: Besides traditional sources like bank loans and equity investors, businesses can explore alternative

funding options. Crowdfunding platforms, grants, government funding, and strategic partnerships are some alternatives worth exploring.

6. Due Diligence: Investors and lenders will conduct thorough due diligence before committing to an investment. Businesses should be prepared to provide detailed financial and operational information to instil confidence in potential investors.

In conclusion, effective financial management and securing funding are critical components of business success. Businesses must implement prudent financial practices, including budgeting, cash flow management, cost control, and financial analysis, to maintain stability and growth. When seeking funding, a well-crafted business plan, targeting the right investors, effective communication, and building strong relationships are essential. By aligning financial management practices with a clear funding strategy, businesses can position themselves for long-term success, growth, and competitiveness in the marketplace.

PART EIGHT

Conclusion

Recap of the 7 Secret Keys to Startup Success

The trip of erecting a successful incipiency is both instigative and gruelling . To navigate this path with confidence and increase the liability of success, entrepreneurs need to unleash the 7 Secret Keys to Startup Success. These keys give precious perceptivity and practicable strategies to overcome hurdles, seize openings, and produce a thriving and sustainable business adventure.

1. relating a Profitable request Gap

The first key is relating to a profitable request gap. Successful startups pinpoint unmet client requirements or underserved requests and develop innovative results to address these gaps. Thorough request exploration, client feedback, and trend analysis are pivotal in understanding the request geography and uncovering openings for dislocation.

2. Casting a Compelling Vision

A compelling vision serves as the North Star of an incipient, guiding its direction and inspiring its platoon. Entrepreneurs should produce a clear and ambitious vision that articulates the long-term pretensions and purpose of the business. A compelling vision attracts talented individualities, motivates stakeholders, and aligns the association towards a common ideal.

3. Developing a Solid Business Plan

A solid business plan is the design for incipiency success. It outlines the business model, target request, profit aqueducts, marketing strategy, and fiscal protrusions. A well- structured business plan not only attracts investors but also provides a roadmap for prosecution and responsibility.

4. erecting a Strong platoon

A incipiency's success heavily relies on the strength of its platoon. Authors should assemble a different and professed platoon that complements each other's strengths. Nurturing a positive and cooperative work culture fosters hand engagement and productivity, leading to collaborative success.

5. Effective Product Development

Developing a product that meets client requirements and exceeds prospects is a critical aspect of incipiency success. exercising nimble methodologies, repeating grounded on client feedback, and conducting thorough product confirmation ensures that the product is aligned with request demands and delights druggies.

6. Financial protrusions and Resource Allocation
Sound fiscal operation is pivotal for incipiency survival and growth. Creating realistic fiscal protrusions, managing cash inflow effectively, and optimising resource allocation enable startups to navigate fiscal challenges and seize growth openings.

7. Marketing and Branding Strategies
Effective marketing and branding strategies are the keys to attract and retain guests. Startups must identify their target followership, produce a compelling brand identity, and develop substantiated marketing juggernauts that reverberate with guests. Building brand fidelity and client advocacy sustains long- term growth.

By unleashing these 7 Secret Keys, entrepreneurs can enhance their chances of incipiency success. Each key complements the others, forming a connected frame that guides startups on their trip. The identification of request gaps leads to the casting of a compelling vision that attracts a strong platoon and lays the foundation for a solid business plan. Effective product development, supported by fiscal protrusions and resource allocation, ensures a product- request fit. Eventually, strategic marketing and branding strategies drive client engagement, energy growth, and solidify the incipiency's position in the business.

Still, success in the incipient world isn't guaranteed. Startups must remain adaptable and flexible, continuously learning from failures, rotating when necessary, and seizing arising openings. Throughout the incipiency trip, perseverance, passion, and a commitment to the charge are essential to overcome challenges and eventually achieve success.

In conclusion, the 7 Secret Keys to Startup Success give a comprehensive frame for entrepreneurs to navigate the gruelling yet satisfying path of erecting a successful incipiency. Relating request gaps, casting a compelling vision, developing a solid business plan, erecting a strong platoon, creating an effective product, managing finances, and enforcing strategic marketing and branding strategies are the foundational rudiments that empower startups to thrive and produce lasting impact in the business. By unleashing these keys and applying them with determination and creativity, entrepreneurs can increase their chances of turning their incipient dreams into reality.

Words of support for aspiring entrepreneurs

To all ambitious entrepreneurs,

Embarking on the entrepreneurial trip is an stirring and gruelling road that requires courage, adaptability, and unwavering drive. As you set out to follow your dreams and bring your ideas to life, know that you're taking a vault of faith into a world of horizonless possibilities and openings for growth. Flash back that success frequently comes to those who accept challenges, learn from failures, and persist with a grim pursuit of their pretensions.

1. Believe in Yourself You retain unique bents, chops, and views that no bone

differently has. Believe in yourself and your capability to turn your idea into reality. Trust your passions and stay true to your passion and purpose. Confidence in yourself and your idea will be the driving force behind your business trip.

2. Embrace Failure as a Stepping Stone Every successful entrepreneur has faced miscalculations and lapses along the way. Embrace failure as a stepping gravestone to success, a precious literacy experience that pushes you near to your pretensions. Failure isn't the end; it's a chance to grow, upgrade your approach, and come back stronger.

3. Seek Support and guidance Do not be hysterical to seek support and guidance from educated entrepreneurs and assistance experts. compass yourself with a network of like-inclined individualities who can offer advice,

share perceptivity, and inspire you to push your limits.

4. Be flexible. The entrepreneurial trip isn't always smooth sailing. There will be challenges, dubieties, and times of query. Embrace these times with adaptability and perseverance. Stay married to your thing, and keep pushing forward indeed when faced with obstacles.

5. acclimatise and introduce The business geography is constantly evolving, and inflexibility is important for survival. Be open to change and introduce your ideas as demanded. Embrace change and seize chances that align with your vision.

6. Focus on client Value At the core of every great business is delivering value to guests. hear your guests' wants and feedback, and let it guide your decision- making process. A client- centric approach will set you piecemeal and promote fidelity.

7. Take Calculated pitfalls Entrepreneurship naturally involves taking pitfalls, but taking advised pitfalls can lead to great prices. Make informed choices grounded on exploration, data, and perceptivity. Do not be hysterical to step out of your comfort zone and take measured hops of faith.

8. Celebrate Small triumphs While it's important to keep your eye on the bigger picture, celebrate the small triumphs along the way. Admitting progress, no matter how small, boosts morale and pushes you to keep moving forward.

9. Focus on Learning and Growth The entrepreneurial trip is a nonstop literacy process. Embrace the chance to learn new chops, gain knowledge, and grow both tête-à-tête and professionally. Invest in your growth to come a better leader and business proprietor.

10. Enjoy the trip Amidst the challenges and hard work, do not forget to enjoy the trip. Celebrate the process, cherish the moments of

alleviation, and take time to admire the mileposts and achievements.

Flash back, the path of an entrepreneur is infrequently smooth, but it's a trip filled with chances for growth, impact, and fulfilment. Embrace the query, embrace the challenges, and embrace your passion for making commodities meaningful. As you start on this remarkable trip, know that the world needs your ideas, your invention, and your unique benefactions.

Believe in yourself, trust the process, and norway lose sight of the effect you can make. With perseverance, fidelity, and a heart full of courage, you have the power to produce your own success story and make a lasting change in the world.

You've got this. conjure big, take action, and make it be!

PART NINE

Appendix

Additional resources and tools

As an aspiring entrepreneur, having access to fresh coffers and tools can significantly enhance your knowledge, chops, and capability to navigate the challenges of starting and growing a successful business. Then are some precious coffers and tools that can support you on your entrepreneurial trip

1. Online Learning Platforms Platforms like Udemy, Coursera, and LinkedIn Learning offer a vast array of courses and tutorials on colourful business motifs, from entrepreneurship and marketing to finance and leadership. These platforms allow you to learn at your own pace and acquire new chops to propel your business forward.

2. Entrepreneurial Communities and Forums Joining entrepreneurial communities and forums, similar as Startup Nation, Reddit's Entrepreneur subreddit, or Quora, provides openings to connect with fellow entrepreneurs, share guests , seek advice, and gain perceptivity from those who have walked an analogous path.

3. Incubators and Accelerators Consider applying to incipiency incubators and accelerators that give mentorship, backing, and networking openings. These programs can give your business a significant boost in its early stages.

4. Business Plan Templates use business plan templates available online to guide you through the process of creating a comprehensive and well- structured business plan. Tools like LivePlan and Bplans offer templates acclimatised to colourful diligence and business types.

5. Financial Management Tools Efficiently managing your finances is pivotal for business success. Tools like QuickBooks, Xero, and FreshBooks help you keep track of your finances, checks, and charges.

6. Project Management Software As your business grows, design operation software like Trello, Asana, orMonday.com can help you stay systematised, manage tasks, and unite with your platoon effectively.

7. Client Relationship Management(CRM) Software CRM tools like HubSpot, Salesforce, or Zoho CRM help in managing client data,

tracking relations, and enhancing client connections.

8. Marketing robotization Marketing robotization platforms like Mailchimp and ActiveCampaign enable you to automate dispatch marketing juggernauts and nurture leads efficiently.

9. Social Media Management Tools like Hootsuite or Buffer help schedule and manage social media posts across multiple platforms, saving time and trouble in your social media marketing sweats.

10. Market Research and Analytics Services like Google Analytics, SEMrush, or SimilarWeb offer precious perceptivity into website business, stoner geste
, and contender analysis, abetting data- driven decision- timber.

11. Design and Creativity Tools Graphic design tools like Canva and Adobe Creative Suite help

produce professional- looking marketing accoutrements and imprinting means.

12. Networking Events and Webinars Attend assistance-specific networking events, webinars, and shops to expand your knowledge, make connections, and stay streamlined on the rearmost trends and stylish practices.

Flash back, nonstop literacy and staying streamlined with assiduity trends are essential for entrepreneurial success. influence these fresh coffers and tools to gain a competitive edge, upgrade your strategies, and stay inspired on your entrepreneurial trip. compass yourself with a probative community, seek mentorship when demanded, and remain married to literacy and growing as an entrepreneur. With fidelity and the right coffers, you can turn your entrepreneurial dreams into a thriving reality.

Worksheets and templates for real application

Worksheets and templates are useful tools for practical application in the world of entrepreneurship. They provide a structured framework to organise thoughts, plan strategies, and make informed choices. Whether you are just starting your business or looking to optimise its operations, these tools can enhance productivity and guide you through critical processes. Here are some key worksheets and templates that can help aspiring entrepreneurs:

1. Business Plan Template: A well-structured business plan is important for any startup. Business plan templates provide a clear outline to document your business idea, target market,

marketing strategies, financial projections, and more. They help you articulate your vision, set goals, and build a roadmap for the future.

2. SWOT Analysis Worksheet:
A SWOT analysis (Strengths, Weaknesses, Opportunities, Threats) helps entrepreneurs measure their business's internal strengths and weaknesses and external opportunities and threats. This analysis enables you to find areas to capitalize on and challenges to address, supporting strategic decision-making.

3. Customer Persona Template: Understanding your target audience is important for successful marketing. Customer persona templates help you build detailed profiles of your ideal customers, including demographics, preferences, pain points, and goals. This knowledge guides your marketing efforts and product development to better serve your audience.

4. Financial Projections Worksheet: Financial projections are important for planning your

business's financial future. Financial projection templates help you to estimate revenues, expenses, profits, and cash flow over a specified time. This info is instrumental in securing funding, setting budgets, and managing financial success.

5. Marketing Plan Template: A marketing plan template outlines your marketing goals, target group, marketing channels, and promotional activities. It serves as a comprehensive guide to executing your marketing strategies and measuring their success.

6. Sales Pipeline Template: A sales pipeline template helps track the progress of possible customers from initial contact to closing a sale. It offers a visual representation of your sales process, enabling you to spot bottlenecks, prioritize leads, and forecast revenue.

7. Project Management Template: For companies working on multiple projects, project management templates streamline planning and

execution. Tools like Gantt charts and task trackers help handle tasks, deadlines, and team collaboration effectively.

8. Cash Flow Forecast Template: A cash flow forecast template helps you to project future cash inflows and outflows. It helps you anticipate potential cash flow gaps and make proactive choices to ensure sufficient liquidity.

9. Social Media Content Calendar: Managing social media can be time-consuming, but a content calendar template allows you to plan and schedule posts in advance. It provides a consistent social media presence and efficient content management.

10. Employee Onboarding Checklist: As your startup grows, hiring and onboarding employees become important. An employee onboarding checklist ensures a smooth shift for new hires, helping them integrate into the company culture and perform their jobs effectively.

11. Performance Review Template: Providing feedback and evaluating employee performance is crucial for employee growth. A performance review template describes key success indicators and encourages constructive conversations.

12. Exit Strategy Template: Thinking about an exit strategy early on is important, even if you're just starting. An exit plan template helps outline possible scenarios and considerations for selling or transitioning out of the business.

These worksheets and templates act as practical tools to streamline processes, enhance organisation, and ease decision-making. As an entrepreneur, incorporating these tools into your workflow can save time, increase productivity, and lead to more informed and successful outcomes. Customise them to suit your business's unique needs, and regularly update them as your business changes. By leveraging these practical resources, you can stay focused on your entrepreneurial journey and make real progress towards your goals.

www.ingramcontent.com/pod-product-compliance
Lightning Source LLC
Chambersburg PA
CBHW070940260726
48661CB00003B/1172